Grade Two

Acoustic Guitar

Accompaniment

Compiled by

The Specialists in Guitar Education

RGT

Registry of Guitar Tutors

www.RGT.org

Printed and bound in Great Britain

A CIP record for this publication is available from the British Library
ISBN: 978-1-905908-42-4

Published by Registry Publications

Registry Mews, Wilton Rd, Bexhill, Sussex, TN40 1HY

Text by Tony Skinner and Merv Young.
All musical compositions by Tony Skinner.
Design by JAK Images.
Front cover photo ©Smileus/Fotolia.
Rear cover photo ©ittipol/Fotolia.

Compiled by

v.20140108

Contents

Page

CD track listing

Track

Introduction

This book is designed primarily to provide supplementary learning materials for candidates preparing for the Accompaniment section of the Registry of Guitar Tutors (RGT) Grade Two acoustic guitar playing exam. However, it should also prove helpful for anyone wishing to develop and improve their accompaniment skills.

Accompaniment is an important skill for any guitarist and is particularly relevant for acoustic guitarists who might be accompanying someone singing (be it themselves or another vocalist) or accompanying another instrumentalist.

In essence, the role of an accompanist is to bring two elements to the overall performance: rhythm and harmony. The chords themselves provide the harmony and the timing of how the chords are played provides the rhythm. In this book the focus is predominantly on the rhythmic elements, as this is where the main decisions are to be made at this level of playing. You will, however, find fretboxes, showing the recommended fingering, for all the new chords required at this level in the Chord Shapes chapter on pages 19 and 20.

This book contains 10 melodies, that have been notated, along with the appropriate chord chart for each one. There are also some tips with each example to get you thinking about how to approach developing your own rhythm playing ideas.

There is also a CD with this book that contains each melody being played on two different tracks. The first CD track for each melody features a guitar playing an example chord accompaniment along with the melody (played twice). The second CD track features the melody on its own (played three times), so that you can play the chords and practise your own accompaniment skills.

Exam Format

In the accompaniment section of the RGT acoustic guitar exams, the candidate is required to play a chordal accompaniment while the examiner plays an eight-bar melody.

In the exam, the candidate will be shown a chord chart for the melody. The examiner will then give a one bar count-in and play the melody once, just for the candidate to listen to without playing along. The examiner will then give another one bar count-in and the melody will be played a further three times without stopping. The candidate can accompany the first of these three verses if they wish to, but only the accompaniment of the second and third verses will be assessed.

Frequently Asked Questions:

Q: In the exam, will I be shown the notation for the melody?
A: No. The melody notation played by the examiner will not be seen by the candidate. This way the candidate can focus on the chord chart and using their musical and aural abilities to create the most appropriate accompaniment.

Q: How will the examiner play the melody?
A: The examiner will play the melody either live on a guitar or keyboard, or via a recording.

Q: Will the examiner give me any advice on how to play the accompaniment?
A: No. The main purpose of this section of the exam is to assess your ability to make musical decisions about the most appropriate way to perform the chords that are presented to you.

Q: Will the examiner let me know when I am supposed to start my playing?
A: The examiner will 'cue you in', although the method of doing so may vary according to the melody being played. As part of your practice with this book, work on being able to follow the chord charts so that you know exactly when to come in by yourself.

Q: What time signature will the chord chart be in?
A: At this grade, all the chord charts will be in $^4_4$ time.

Q: Which chords will occur in the chord chart?
A: The range of chords that may occur at this grade are listed in the Chord Charts chapter of this book.

Q: How many chords will appear in each chord chart?
A: At this grade, there will be five *different* chords in each chord chart. Three of the chords in each sequence will last for two bars; the remaining chords will last for one bar each. In the very final bar (after the repeat) the chord should be played with a single strum.

Accompaniment Advice

In the exam, the style of the accompaniment is left to the candidate's discretion, and the candidate can chose to either strum or fingerpick. The CD demo recordings that are provided with this book are intended to give an indication of the technical level that would be expected for a high mark at this grade. (Note that only the two assessed verses are provided in each accompaniment demo recording.) To ensure that you can clearly hear the accompaniment guitar part on the CD demo tracks, the level of the accompaniment guitar has deliberately been made louder than would normally occur in a standard recording. The demo recordings of the accompaniment parts are not intended to provide exact templates for candidates to copy; they are provided as examples of the standard required, and candidates are strongly encouraged to devise their own rhythmic/picking styles.

The demo recordings also provide an insight into the factors that need to be considered when developing accompaniment ideas. When accompanying, each melody can be interpreted in a number of ways and there will be a range of playing techniques and rhythm styles that can be effectively adopted. The aim of this book is to enable the player to start developing their playing skills so that sympathetic musical decisions can be made to both support and enhance the melody being played. In general, it will be possible for the chords to be played in a range of styles including: strumming using a combination of downstrokes and upstrokes; using simple arpeggiated patterns with either the fingers or a plectrum (pick); using a specific musical playing style, such as a continuous downstroke strumming pattern.

Accompaniment Tips

1. Your playing should always relate to the timing and style of the melody played by the examiner.

2. Remember that the very first time the examiner plays the melody, you have the opportunity to listen to it without needing to play along. Use this opportunity to listen carefully and try to absorb the melodic shape and structure of the melody.

3. In the first verse of the three continuous playings your playing will not be assessed, so you can best use this time by reading through the chord chart and just strumming once on the first beat of each bar so that the timing becomes clearly fixed in your mind.

4. In the remaining two verses use an appropriate rhythm or picking style that suits the mood, style and timing of the melody. When you are practising the examples in this book, keep experimenting to develop your own musical ideas. Listen out for any prominent rhythmic elements of the melody that you can respond to and emulate with the chords. For instance, if the melody has a strong 1 2&3 4 rhythm to it, you could replicate this with your rhythm playing. Alternatively, if there is a bar with only one melody note, you might choose to play a busier rhythm in this bar to create a musical contrast.

5. Keep listening closely to the melody while playing your accompaniment and make sure to keep in time with it. Practice carefully to ensure that your chords come in on the first beat of each bar, to help establish a definite pulse and rhythm.

6. Ensure that you are totally comfortable with playing all the chord shapes on their own before you attempt them with the accompaniment practice track. There are several new chords introduced at this grade, some of which may prove tricky at first, so practise these carefully and separately. In order to ensure that the chords sound clearly, make sure that your fretting fingers are as close to the frets as they can be.

7. Use your knowledge of the chord shapes to change smoothly from one chord to another, whilst making sure your chords ring clear. It might be that the strumming is fluent but the chord changes are not as smooth as they need to be. In that case, initially try playing along with one of the example melodies but just strumming each chord once – to give yourself more time to change onto the next chord. (Remember that this advice is only for practising the chord changes, not how to play in the exam itself.) As this becomes comfortable, try strumming each chord twice and build up from there until you have the confidence to play the full strumming pattern.

8. Take time to listen to how the chords themselves sound. It is very easy to get too wrapped up in the fingering and chord shapes and not listen carefully to the actual sound being produced. Are all the strings ringing out clearly? Is there buzzing from any of the fretted notes?

9. At this level it's important to include some variation of your rhythm pattern in the final verse. Think about ways to develop your original strumming pattern ideas as you are playing with the practice tracks. See if you can incorporate some variations as you are playing along and listen out for points where some variation will be particularly effective, for instance, in the final bar before the sequence repeats. If this doesn't work at first, try your ideas on their own, without the practice track, and then have another go. The more you practise this, the more instinctive this ability will become.

10. If you make a mistake whilst playing the accompaniment, DO NOT STOP. It is important for the overall musical result that you keep playing (something – anything!) so that you do not lose your place in the music and fall out of time with the melody. Regardless of what mistake you might make with a chord shape, it will never sound worse than if you come to a complete stop – particularly as the melody will carry on without you. If you cannot change to a chord in time, then simply place your fretting hand across the strings to mute them whilst you carry on strumming – it's not ideal, but it will definitely sound preferable to a total halt and the risk of losing your co-ordination with the melody.

Chord Charts

Examples of the type of chord charts that will occur in the Accompaniment section of the Grade Two RGT acoustic guitar playing exam are given on the following pages. Note that these chord charts are provided only as examples of *the types* of chord charts that may occur in the exam.

The new chords that may occur at this grade are:

Amaj7 Cmaj7 Dmaj7 Fmaj7 Gmaj7   Am7 Dm7 Em7   F   C7 G7

Fretboxes showing the suggested fingering for these chords are provided at the back of this book. You do not have to use the same fingering as shown in this book or in the exam handbook; any alternative chord fingerings will be acceptable, provided the chords are musically correct.

In addition, the chords from previous grades may also occur in the chord charts for this grade:

A C D E G   Am Dm Em   A7 B7 D7 E7

Please study the earlier book in this series if you are not familiar with any of these lower grade chords.

Below each example chord chart in this chapter, the melody, that it is designed to accompany, is provided in both standard notation and tablature. Note that in the exam itself, the melody will NOT be shown to the candidate; it is provided in this book purely for situations where a teacher might wish to play the melody with a student rather than use the CD provided.

A sample rhythm pattern has been notated below each chord chart in this chapter; this is the rhythm pattern that is predominantly used on the demonstration track, which provides an example of the standard expected for a very high mark at this grade. Each rhythm pattern has been designed to reflect some of the main rhythmic features of the melody. During the second verse the rhythm pattern used in the first verse is largely repeated, with just some slight variations. Such variations are optional at this grade level, and are included primarily to demonstrate that it is not necessary to exactly replicate the rhythms used in the first verse during the second verse. The rhythm pattern can be used as a starting point for your own rhythm playing. However, for each chord chart, this will be just one of many different interpretations that are possible and you are encouraged to explore and practise different rhythm patterns so as to develop your accompaniment skill and your ability to reflect the main rhythmic elements of a melody.

For each example on the following pages there are some specific tips and advice that are relevant to that chord chart and melody. Use these as ideas from which to start developing your own interpretations. The advice is intended to help you to develop your own skills and confidence in this area of playing.

Chord Chart 1 (CD Track 1)

$\frac{4}{4}$	Am		Am		Fmaj7		Fmaj7	

Em7		Em7		G		E7		Am	

On the demonstration track the following rhythm pattern is played in the first of every two bars:

The melody for this example has a fairly relaxed feel to it so the rhythm pattern is reflective of this. The eighth notes that occur after beats 1 and 2 are played with upstrokes on the demonstration track, with the remaining notes being played with downstrokes. This strumming pattern reflects the melody that is played in bars 1, 3, 5 and 7, with the upstrokes helping to emphasise the relaxed nature of the melody.

On the demonstration track, bars 2, 4, 6 and 8 are generally played with a simpler four-to-the-bar strumming pattern, with some slight variation during the second verse. Whichever rhythm pattern you use, don't lose sight of the overall essence of the melody by keeping the rhythm and strumming light and stylistically appropriate.

Melody 1 (CD Track 2)

Chord Chart 2 (CD Track 3)

$\left\|\frac{4}{4}\right\|$: **D** |**D** |**A** |**A** |

|**G**maj7 |**G**maj7 |**E**m |**A7**   :‖**D**   ‖

On the demonstration track the following rhythm pattern is played over many of the bars:

This melody has a strong riff-based feel to it, which is reflected in the strumming pattern. On the demonstration track this is played using downstrokes and upstrokes, with the upstroke being played on the off-beat that occurs after beat 3: Down Down DownUpDown.

To create more drive and energy try playing this pattern with downstrokes throughout. You might also try varying the rhythm in bars 7 and 8 to help generate extra interest and rhythmic momentum before the melody repeats, or before the melody ends. For instance, try playing 8 eighth note strums over the A7 chord in bar 8 before playing the final D chord – a very effective device to end a performance with. There are some examples of rhythmic variation demonstrated in bars 7 and 8 on the demonstration track during the second verse, so listen carefully to get an idea of what you can try here.

Melody 2 (CD Track 4)

Chord Chart 3 (CD Track 5)

On the demonstration track the chords are often played with the following rhythm:

The melody here is quite lively and the strumming pattern is picking up on some of the elements of the melody's rhythm. The eighth note that occurs after beat 4 is played with an upstroke on the demonstration track and this doesn't leave you with much time to change chord – especially challenging at this faster tempo. Use this example as an opportunity to practise the chord changes until they are smooth and fluent. Try to keep your strumming hand moving constantly whilst you change chords – don't stop strumming and wait for your fretting hand to assemble the chord shape or you'll lose momentum and fluency.

There are a number of strumming pattern variations that could prove effective, as you'll hear demonstrated on the track. In some bars, a sparser strumming pattern has been adopted to act as a contrast, as well as some other variations to the main rhythm pattern.

Melody 3 (CD Track 6)

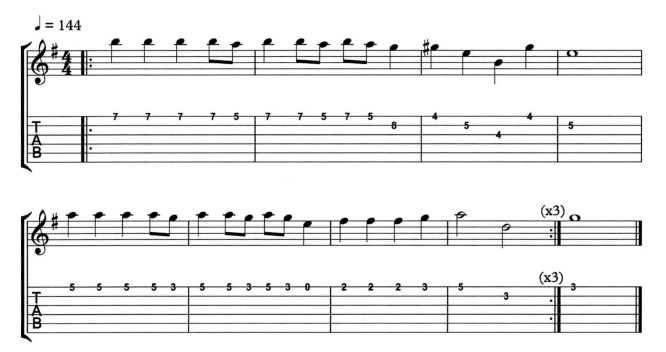

Chord Chart 4 (CD Track 7)

| $\frac{4}{4}$ ‖: E | | E | | Amaj7 | | Amaj7 | |

| E | | A | | B7 | | B7 | :‖ E | | ‖

On the demonstration track the following rhythm pattern is played during the first verse:

In this example, the melody features a relatively straightforward rhythm. To enhance this, the strumming pattern for the chords is busier, featuring eighth notes being played on beats 2 and 3. On the demonstration track a combination of downstrokes and upstrokes is used: Down DownUpDownUpDown.

In the second verse, some slight rhythmic variations are used to enrich the overall musical effect and prevent the strumming sounding too repetitive.

There are several new chords introduced at this grade which will take some practice until they become familiar. When changing from the E to the Amaj7 chord try to keep the first finger held down on fret 1 of the G (3rd) string as this note is the same for both chords. This 'minimum movement' technique will help to improve the fluency of your chord changes.

Melody 4 (CD Track 8)

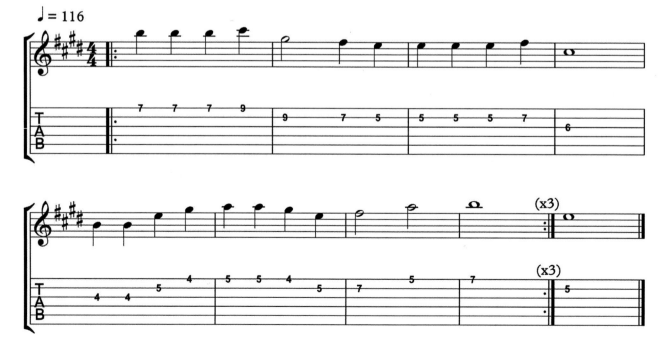

12

Chord Chart 5 (CD Track 9)

 **G** | **G**maj7 | **C** | **C** |

| **A**m7 | **A**m7 | **D7** | **D7** :| **G** ‖

On the demonstration track the chords are played with the following rhythm in several of the bars:

You'll notice that this strumming pattern reflects the distinctive rhythm that occurs in bars 1, 2, 5 and 6 of the melody. The rhythm of the melody in these bars includes some 'syncopation', where instead of beat 3 being emphasised, the melody is phrased to emphasise the off-beat just after beat 2. This type of syncopation is very common in many styles of popular music. On the demonstration track this rhythm is played with downstrokes and upstrokes as follows: Down DownUp UpDown.

The other bars of the melody are simpler, and a more straightforward 1 2& 3 4& rhythm pattern is generally used in those bars. Of course, there is plenty of scope to experiment here. For instance, in the penultimate bar you could try the following pattern played entirely with downstrokes to help generate some momentum and drive prior to the final chord ending:

Melody 5 (CD Track 10)

♩ = 104

Chord Chart 6 (CD Track 11)

$\frac{4}{4}$ | A | **A**maj7 | **D**maj7 | **D**maj7 | |

| **E** | **E** | **D** | **D** | **A** | |

On the demonstration track the chords are played with the following rhythm throughout the first verse:

The rhythm pattern reflects the prominent and repeated main rhythmic element of the melody that, like the previous track, includes some 'syncopation' in that the off-beat just after beat 2 is emphasised rather than beat 3. On the demonstration track this rhythm pattern is played using a combination of downstrokes and upstrokes as follows: Down DownUp UpDown.

In bars 4, 6 and 8, where the melody is sparser, you could try some variations to this rhythm pattern. For instance, you could adopt a simpler pattern that reflects the melody in these bars. You'll hear some variation ideas on the demonstration track during the second verse.

Melody 6 (CD Track 12)

14

Chord Chart 7 (CD Track 13)

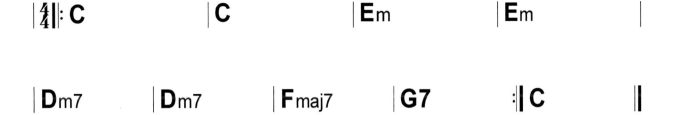

On the demonstration track the chords are played with the following rhythm in most of the bars:

Like the previous melody, this melody is 'syncopated' and emphasises the off-beat after beat 2 (rather than the more expected beat 3). The strumming pattern draws on the main rhythmic element of the melody that appears in bars 1, 3, 5 and 7. Although the rhythm of the melody in the remaining bars is simpler, maintaining the same syncopated strumming pattern helps to maintain a sense of momentum and pulse. However, on the demonstration track, to add a little contrast, some differing rhythmic variations are played in bar 8 during each verse.

On the demonstration track, the main pattern is played with a combination of downstrokes and upstrokes as follows: DownUpDownUp UpDown. However, experiment with the use of more downstrokes (for instance, DownUpDownDown DownDown) as this can be an effective way to create a stronger sound in certain bars. Experiment to see what you prefer and what sounds effective.

Melody 7 (CD Track 14)

Chord Chart 8 (CD Track 15)

| 4/4 ‖: A7 | A7 | C7 | C7 | |

| D7 | D7 | E | E7 :‖ A7 | ‖ |

On the demonstration track the chords are played with the following rhythm pattern throughout the first verse:

The small arrow heads underneath some of the notes are 'accent' marks, which mean that the chords should be emphasised a little more on these beats. You'll hear this on the demonstration track and you'll also notice that the rhythm is played with downstrokes throughout. This helps to emphasise the effect of these accents, as well as assisting in driving the rhythm forward to accompany this lively, riff-based melody. On the demonstration track you'll hear that bars 7 and 8 feature a slightly different rhythm pattern during the second verse, while still maintaining this accented feel.

You could try experimenting with the placement of the accents. Make sure you can comfortably play them as indicated first and then see if you can accent different parts of the bar to develop this useful playing technique.

Melody 8 (CD Track 16)

Chord Chart 9 (CD Track 17)

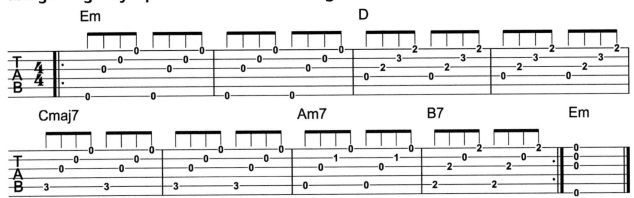

$\frac{4}{4}$ |: **E**m | **E**m | **D** | **D** |

| **C**maj7 | **C**maj7 | **A**m7 | **B**7 :|| **E**m ||

On the demonstration track for this example you'll notice that the chords are played using a fingerstyle pattern rather than being strummed.

This features a steady eighth note pattern throughout that provides a smooth backdrop for the melody to play over. On the demonstration track, during the first verse, the bass note of each chord is played first with the thumb, followed by strings 3, 2 and 1 using three different fingers with the picking hand. To create a contrast for the ending, a reversed finger pattern (with string order 5123) is used in bars 7 and 8 during the second verse. These patterns can also be played effectively by using a pick (plectrum) to play each individual note. It's a good idea to fret the entire chord shape even if you aren't intending to play those notes in your pattern; that way you'll be still playing notes from the correct chord even if your picking hand accidently strikes a different string. In the exam, there is no requirement to play an accompaniment fingerstyle; you could strum a suitable rhythm instead.

Melody 9 (CD Track 18)

♩ = 100

Chord Chart 10 (CD Track 19)

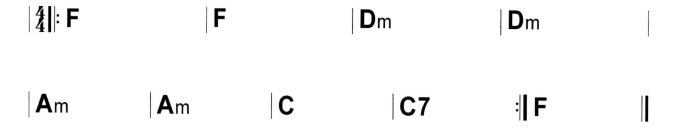

On the demonstration track for this example you'll notice that the chords are played using a fingerstyle pattern, rather than being strummed. For this style of playing hold down the required chord shape with the fretting hand whilst the picking hand plays the pattern indicated.

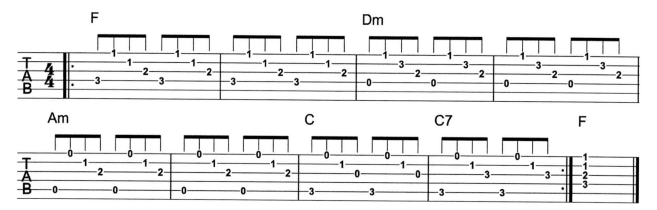

On the demonstration track the bass note of each pattern is played using the thumb of the picking hand, with the top three strings then being picked in descending order with three different fingers. This could be played equally as effectively using a pick (plectrum) to play each individual note in the chord, so try both methods to see which feels more comfortable for you. Notice how a variation in the picking pattern is used at the end of the 2nd verse.

Melody 10 (CD Track 20)

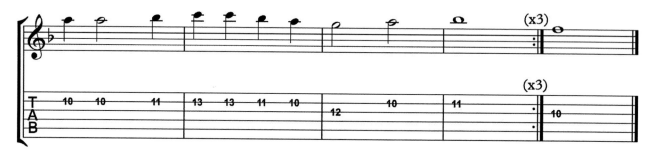

18

Chord Shapes

This chapter provides the fingering for the full range of chords that may occur in the Accompaniment section of the Grade Two RGT acoustic guitar playing exam.

If, in the exam, you prefer to use an alternative fingering, for any chord, that would be perfectly acceptable, providing the pitches are all accurate and an effective musical result is produced.

In addition to the chords shown below, you will need to know the following chords from lower grades:

A, C, D, E, G   **Am, Dm, Em**   **A7, B7, D7, E7**

Please consult the Grade One book in this series if you are unsure about any of these chords.

F   C7   G7

Am7
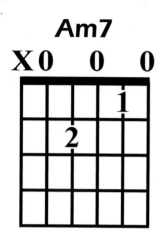

Dm7
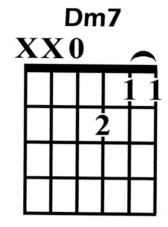

Em7
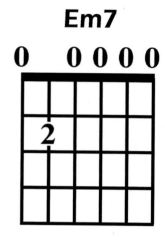

Amaj7
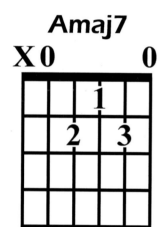

Cmaj7
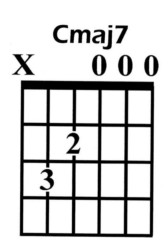

Dmaj7
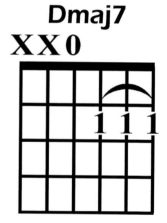

Fmaj7
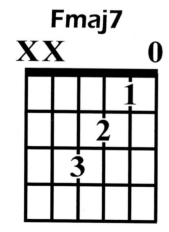

Gmaj7
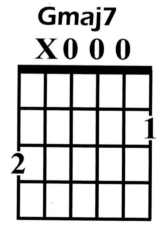